Basic Tips & Instructions for Succ

Just follow our Never-fail instructions to p... wood pieces easily with ZIG™ Woodcraft Markers f... give as gifts to special friends.

Basic Materials:

ZIG™ Woodcraft Markers	Wood pieces
Tracing and Transfer paper	Stylus or pencil
Goop glue or Lo temp glue	Spray finish

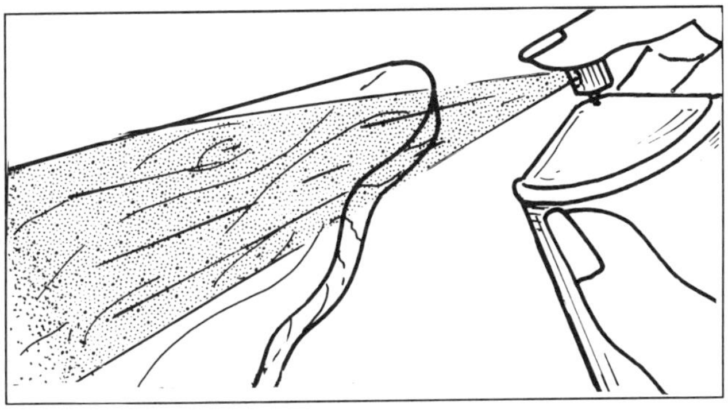

1. Sand & Seal pine wood pieces with water based sealer. Hardwood pieces do not require sealing.

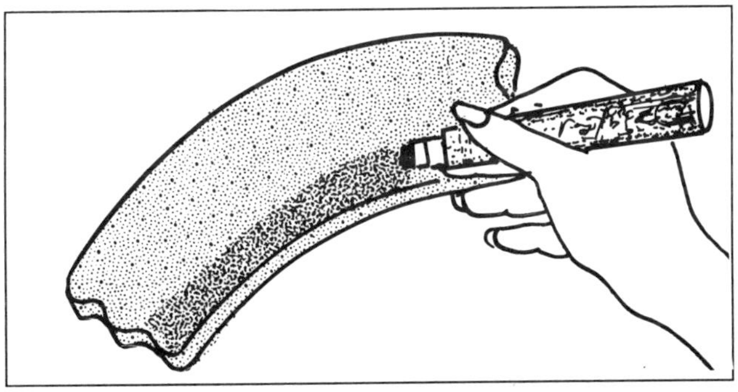

2. Basecoat with Big & Broad Woodcraft Markers. Two coats may be necessary when covering large areas. Paint with long, even strokes in the direction of the wood grain.

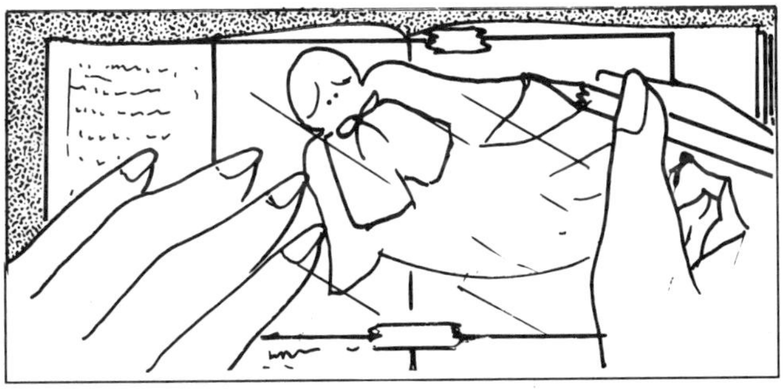

3. Trace and Transfer Pattern. Trace pattern on tracing paper. Place transfer paper between pattern and wood. Trace over pattern with a pencil or stylus.

Additional Materials:

Loew-Cornell #4 flat brush Series 797	
DecoArt matte spray finish	DecoArt gel stain
Water based sealer	18 gauge wire
Raffia	Craft drill

Note: ZIG™ Woodcraft Markers have a remarkably opaque quality and mistakes can be easily corrected by painting over.

4. Paint design with Chisel Tip Marker. Paint lettering using the corner of a Chisel Tip Marker or Extra Fine Tip Marker. Add details with an Extra Fine Tip Marker. Always let one color dry before adding another color. If tip seems to dry out, press gently to release more paint.

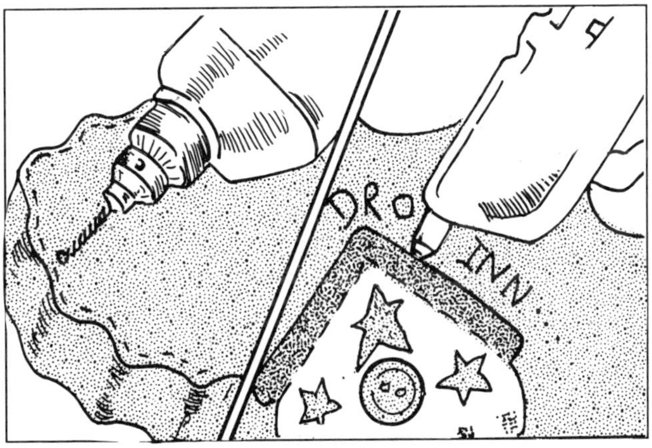

5. Finish. Make holes with craft drill. Glue pieces together with lo-temp glue or GOOP glue. Spray with sealer.

Painting Techniques

1. Use large area of marker to fill in color.
2. Use edge of marker to paint narrow lines.
3. Use corner of marker to paint dots or lettering.
4. Pull marker down in a vertical direction for narrow stripes and in a horizontal direction for wider stripes.
5. Stipple with tip of Extra Fine marker.

1.

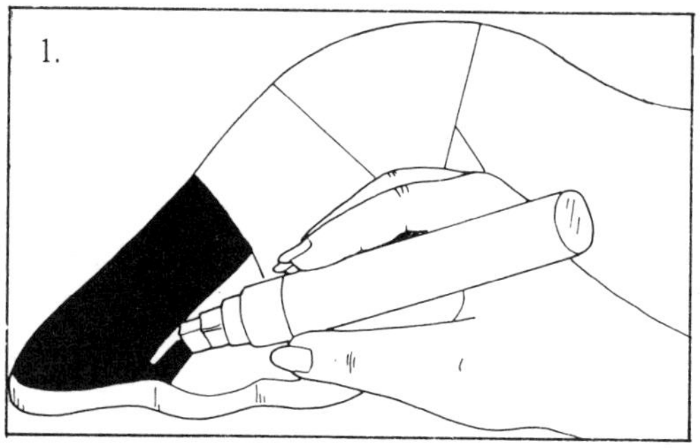

2.

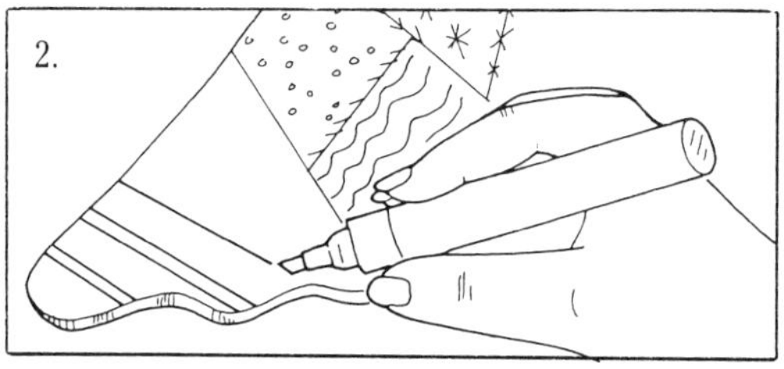

3.

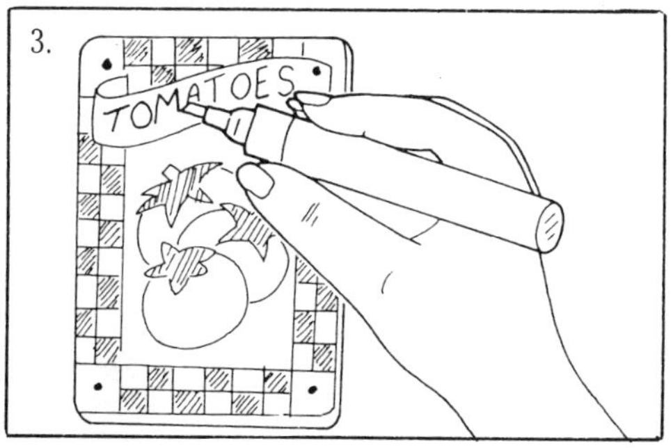

4.

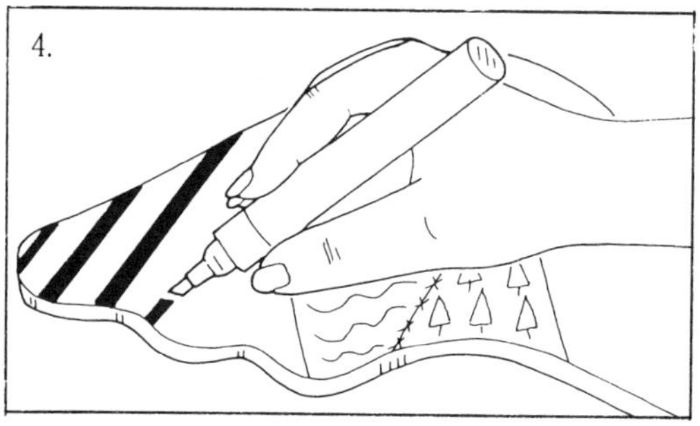

5.

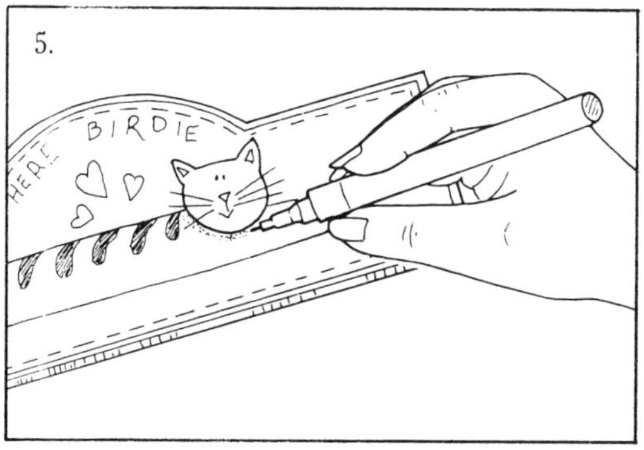

FLOAT TECHNIQUE - To shade and highlight, scribble a small amount of the shading color on a hard surface such as a glass plate. Dip a flat brush in water and pat on a paper towel to remove excess water. Stroke the corner of the brush through the color then paint area to be shaded or highlighted.
NOTE: The paint from the markers dries very quickly, so it will have to be frequently renewed when shading larger areas.

ANTIQUE - Paint project with markers, allow to dry. Spray with sealer. When dry, cover with Walnut gel stain. Wipe off with soft cloth..

WASH TECHNIQUE - To wash, scribble a small amount of the shading color on a hard surface such as a glass plate. Dip a flat brush in water and shake off excess water. Mix with color. Paint over basecoat to lightly tint.

Marker Sizes and Uses

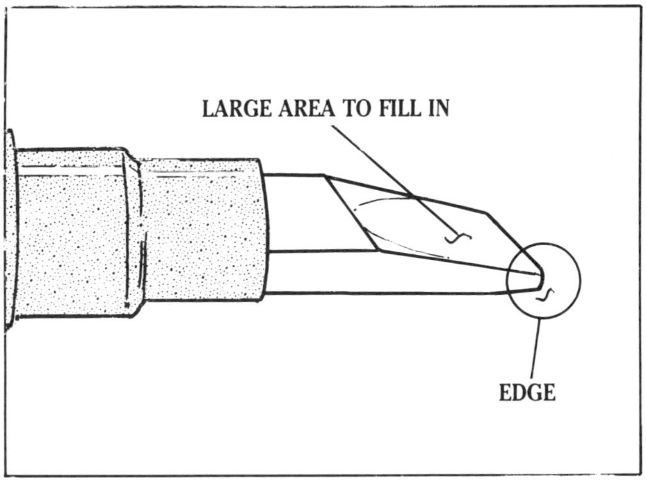

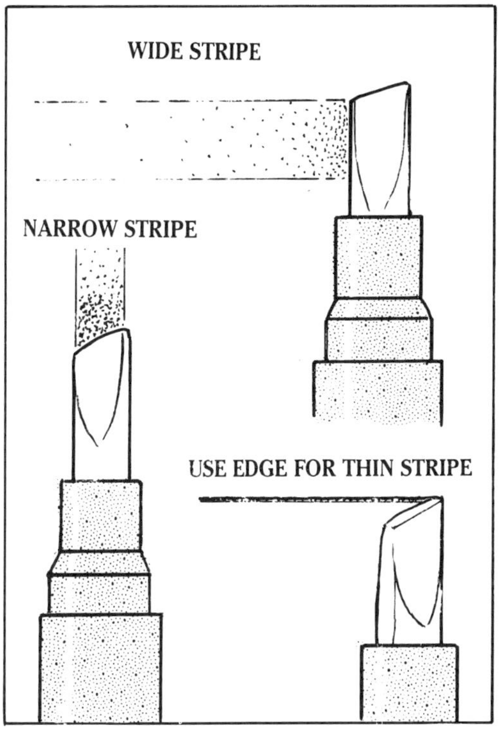

Shake markers to mix the paint.
Press tip gently on a hard surface to release the paint.

NOTE: If the paint begins to dry out in the tip, press again *once* or *twice* only to release more paint. DO NOT pump repeatedly or pen will flood.

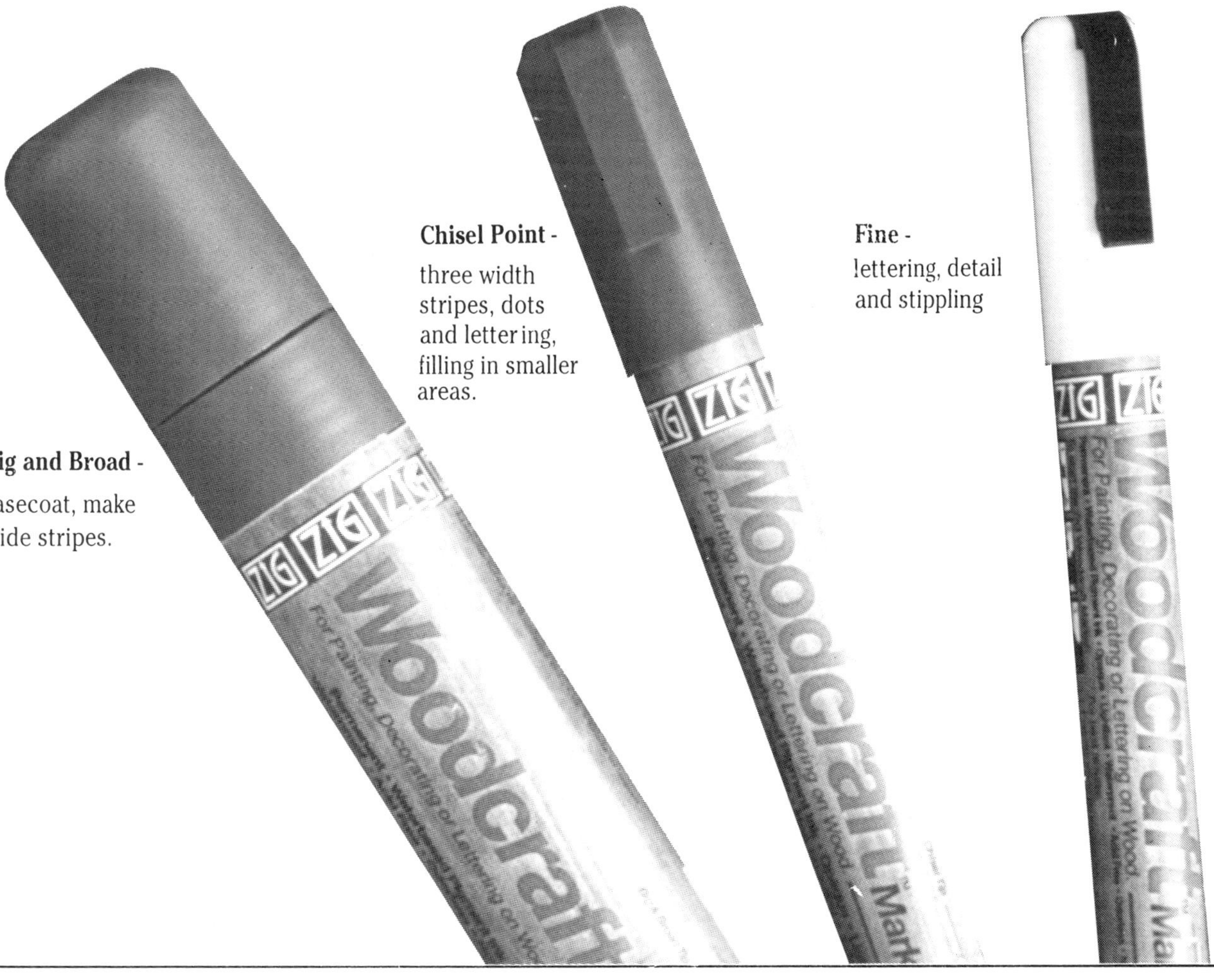

Chisel Point - three width stripes, dots and lettering, filling in smaller areas.

Fine - lettering, detail and stippling

Big and Broad - basecoat, make wide stripes.

Patchwork Angel

FRONT COVER PHOTO

MATERIALS:

Earth Angel
Large primitive star
Small chunky heart (bird)
18" of wire
Gray moss
Dried baby's breath
Raffia
Soft cloth
DecoArt Walnut Gel Stain

ZIG WOODCRAFT MARKERS:

Extra Fine - Black, Arctic White, Gold Metallic
Chisel Tip - Flesh, Crimson, True Blue, Burnt Sienna, Peacock, Slate Gray, Yellow, Bright Green, Forest Green, Pumpkin, Arctic White

INSTRUCTIONS:

Sand and seal wood.
Trace and transfer pattern.

PAINT:

Face - Flesh, shade Burnt Sienna.
  Eyes - Arctic White, True Blue and Black.
  Cheeks - shade Crimson.
  Mouth - Crimson, shade - Burnt Sienna. Outline Black.
Patches
  Peacock - True Blue and Slate Gray stripes.
  Yellow - dot Crimson.
  Flesh - line Arctic White.
  Arctic White - Gold Metallic stars.
  Bright Green - Forest Green triangle, outline Black. Add Burnt Sienna trunk.
  Pumpkin - Burnt Sienna swirls.
Star - Yellow, shade outer edge Pumpkin.
Bird - Crimson, shade Black.
  Eye - dot Black.

FINISH:
Spray with sealer. Antique angel with Walnut gel stain. Drill hole in top of head and edge of star. Attach wire to star, curl around dowel and glue other end in top of head. Glue moss to head and bird in moss. Glue flowers around front. Tie raffia bow and glue to front under head. Attach wire to holes in wings, curl ends to secure.

Funky Plaid Angel

CENTER PHOTO

MATERIALS:
Small apple (head)
3 medium primitive hearts (wings)
2 arms
2 split wren eggs (feet)
Dome (body)
Two 5" pieces of wire (legs)
6" of wire
3" of Brass wire
Excelsior

ZIG WOODCRAFT MARKERS:
Extra Fine - Black
Chisel Tip - Yellow, Flesh, Crimson, Bright Green, Rust, Forest Green, Peacock

INSTRUCTIONS:

PAINT:
Wings (2 hearts) - Yellow, outline and dash Black.
Body - Bright Green.
  Horizontal stripes - Forest Green.
  Vertical stripes - Rust.
  Lines - Black.
Arms - Bright Green.
  Edge of sleeve - Forest Green.
  Outline - Black.
  Hands - Flesh.
Head - Flesh.
  Cheeks - Crimson, dot Arctic White.
  Eyes - Black.
Feet - Flesh.
  Shoes - Rust.
  Bows - Black.
Heart - Crimson.
  Patch - Peacock.
  Details - Black.

FINISH:
Drill holes in corners of wings, heart, right hand and bottom of dome. Glue excelsior to head and head to top of dome. Glue arms to front of dome and wings to back. Curl 5" pieces of wire. Attach one end to bottom of dome and one end to feet. Attach Red heart to wire, curl and attach to hand. Make halo using Brass wire, glue on head. Attach 6" wire to holes in wings for hanger.

Summer Pot

CENTER PHOTO
MATERIALS:
4" x 4" terra cotta pot
ZIG WOODCRAFT MARKERS:
Big & Broad - Arctic White, True Blue
Extra Fine - Black
Chisel Tip - Crimson, Yellow, Burnt Sienna, Arctic White, Forest Green
INSTRUCTIONS:
Trace and transfer pattern.
PAINT:
Edge - Arctic White and True Blue, shade True Blue.
Heart - Crimson.
Outline hearts, edges of checks - small Black dashes and X's.
Sunflower - Yellow.
  Center - Burnt Sienna.
  Crosshatch - Black, add Arctic White dots.
  Details - stipple around center and outline Black.
  Leaves - Forest Green, outline Black.
FINISH:
Spray with sealer.

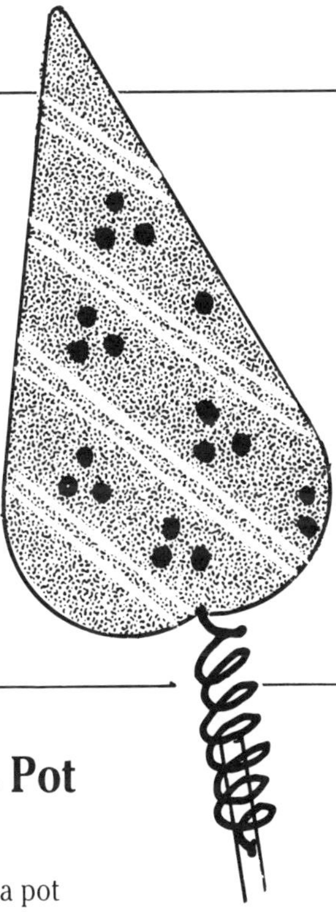

Folk Heart Pick

CENTER PHOTO
MATERIALS:
$2\frac{3}{4}$" primitive heart
9" of wire
3" of $\frac{3}{8}$" dowel
ZIG WOODCRAFT MARKERS:
Extra Fine - Arctic White
Chisel Tip - Bright Green, Crimson
PAINT:
Heart - Bright Green. Add Crimson dots and Arctic White stripes.
FINISH:
Drill hole in top of heart, attach one end of wire. Curl remaining wire around dowel. Attach wire to dowel.

Christmas Pot

CENTER PHOTO
MATERIALS:
4" x 6" terra cotta pot
1 yard of jute
ZIG WOODCRAFT MARKERS:
Extra Fine - Black, Arctic White
Chisel Tip - Forest Green, Bright Green, Crimson, Burnt Sienna
INSTRUCTIONS:
Trace and transfer pattern.
PAINT:
Large trees - Forest Green with Bright Green stripes. Add Crimson dots with Arctic White dots.
  Trunk - Burnt Sienna
Small trees - Bright Green. Add Arctic White dots.
  Trunk - Burnt Sienna.
Details - outline Black.
FINISH:
Spray with sealer. Wrap jute around top of pot twice, tie a bow.

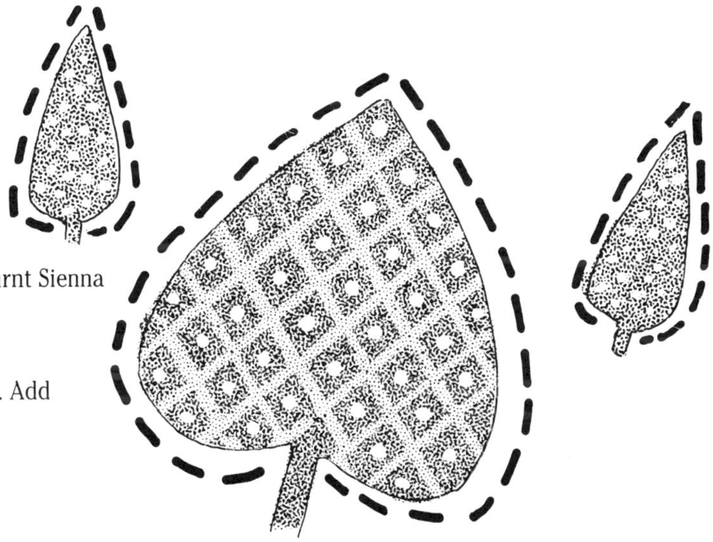

Bird Lady

CENTER PHOTO

ZIG WOODCRAFT MARKERS:
Big & Broad - Arctic White
Extra Fine - Black, Arctic White
Chisel Tip - Rust, Victorian Blue, Crimson, Flesh, Forest Green, Black, Yellow

MATERIALS:
$\frac{3}{4}$" x 6" piece of Yellow check fabric (ribbon)
1" x 9" piece Red plaid fabric (scarf)
12" of wired greenery
12" twig bundle
20" of $\frac{3}{16}$" dowel
Two 9" strands of raffia
Grey moss
Pink cosmetic blush
Toothpicks (small bird beaks)
18" of wire

WOOD PARTS:
Mini tall arch clock (body)
Christmas tree (hair)
Optional: Large Primitive Star
Five $\frac{1}{4}$" beads (small birds)
2 birdhouses
Split pigeon egg (head)
2 mittens (hands)
2 stockings (feet)
Bird
Watering can

INSTRUCTIONS:
Trace patterns.

PAINT:
Body - Arctic White. Shade Rust along bottom edge.
Transfer pattern.
Hole - Rust, shade Rust around outer edges.
  Patches - Victorian Blue rectangle with Arctic White stripes.
  Heart - Crimson with Black stitches.
Feet - Black, highlight Arctic White.
Hands - Crimson.
  Patch - Forest Green.
  Outline - Black.
Bird - Black.
  Beak - Yellow.
  Outline - Arctic White dashes.
Watering can - Forest Green, shade Black.
Birdhouse A - Crimson.
  Roof - Black, shade Black.
  Center hole - Black, add Black dashes.
  Stars - True Blue, outline Black.
Birdhouse B - Arctic White.
  Roof, bottom edge - Forest Green, shade Rust.
  Hole - Black.
  Checks - Rust.
  Checks, roof, hole - outline Black.
Hair - Rust and Black.
Head - Flesh.
  Eyes, mouth - Black.
  Cheeks - rub with blush.
Baby birds - Black.
  Beaks - Yellow toothpicks.
Dowel - Flesh.

DRILL HOLES:
  Each side of clock for arms.
  Bottom of clock for legs.
  End of hands.
  Top of feet.
  Bottom of bird.
  Top of left hand
  Handle of watering can.
  Top of birdhouses.
  Three along edge of feet.
  Top of clock $\frac{1}{4}$" from front edge.
  Bottom of head.
Cut dowel into one 1", two 4" and two 6" pieces.

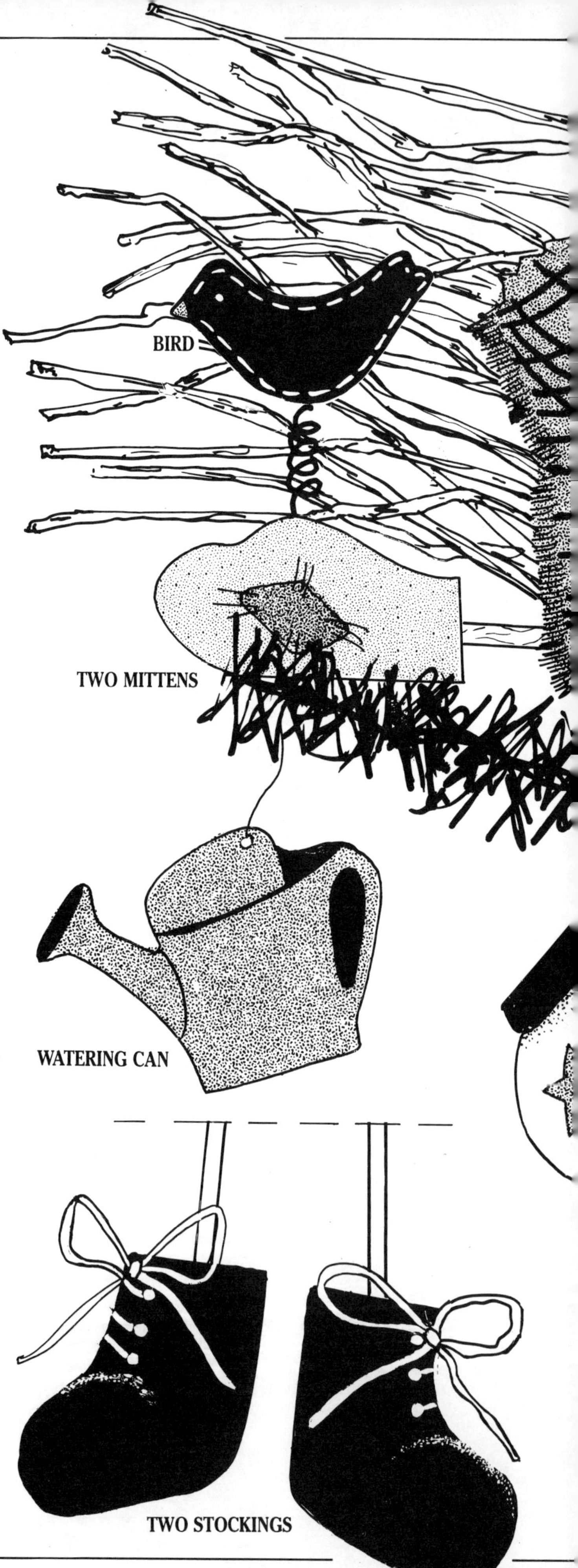

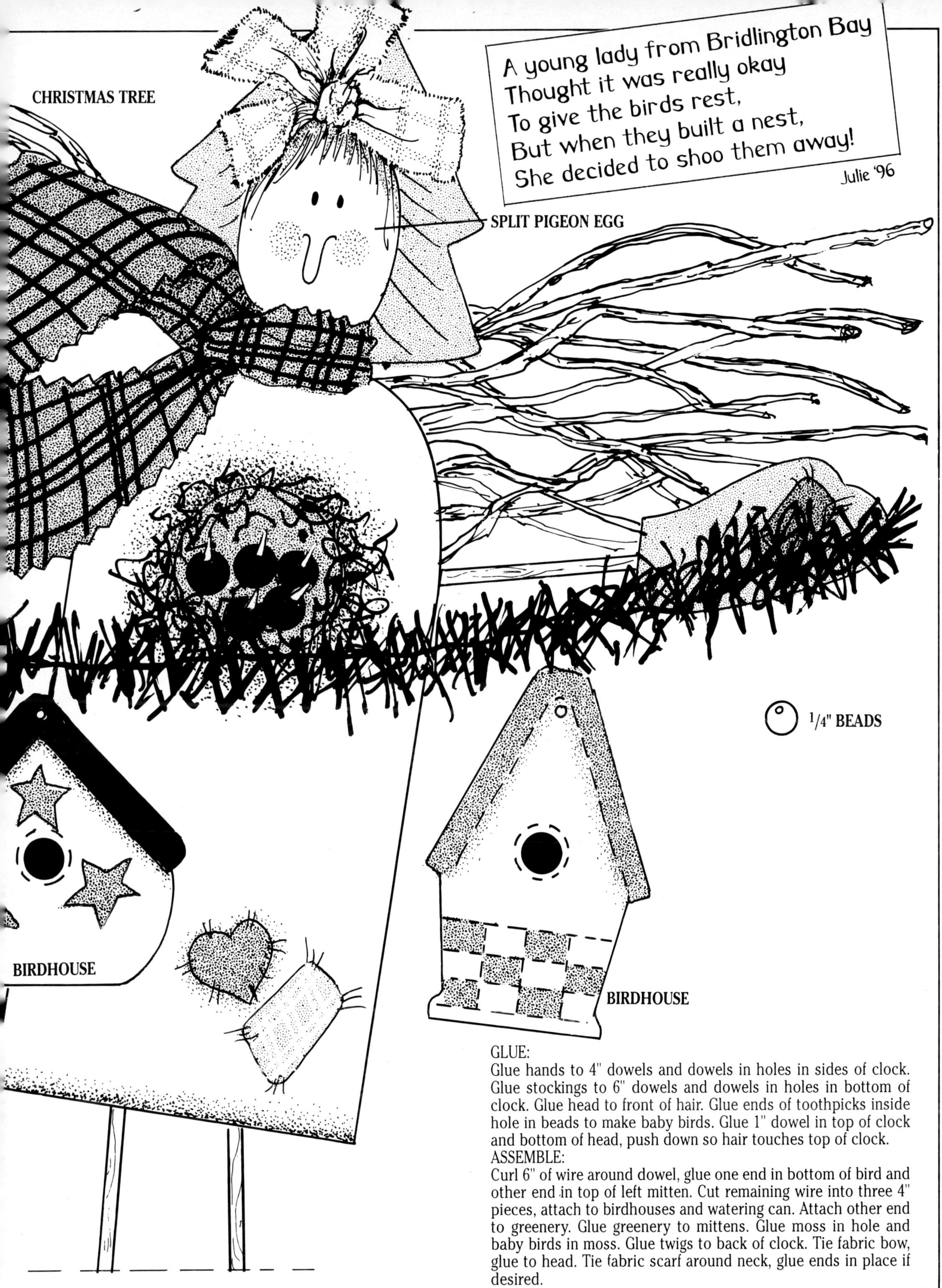

A young lady from Bridlington Bay
Thought it was really okay
To give the birds rest,
But when they built a nest,
She decided to shoo them away!
Julie '96

GLUE:
Glue hands to 4" dowels and dowels in holes in sides of clock. Glue stockings to 6" dowels and dowels in holes in bottom of clock. Glue head to front of hair. Glue ends of toothpicks inside hole in beads to make baby birds. Glue 1" dowel in top of clock and bottom of head, push down so hair touches top of clock.
ASSEMBLE:
Curl 6" of wire around dowel, glue one end in bottom of bird and other end in top of left mitten. Cut remaining wire into three 4" pieces, attach to birdhouses and watering can. Attach other end to greenery. Glue greenery to mittens. Glue moss in hole and baby birds in moss. Glue twigs to back of clock. Tie fabric bow, glue to head. Tie fabric scarf around neck, glue ends in place if desired.

You'll love using Zig® Woodcraft Markers to color ever
decorations and garden pots. Fine point, medium an

ing from birdhouses, to angels, wall hangings, holiday
iant tips make decorating easy enough for beginners.

Mr. Noah's Boat Rides

CENTER PHOTO

MATERIALS:
10" square frame
Mini sign
Ark
5" square of canvas paper
Toothpick
18" of jute
18" of wire
DecoArt Walnut Gel Stain
Soft cloth
Sanding sponge

ZIG WOODCRAFT MARKERS:
Big & Broad - True Blue
Extra Fine - Black, Arctic White
Chisel Tip - Crimson, Pumpkin, Forest Green, Bright Green, Rust, Slate Gray, Carnation Pink, Arctic Ice, Burnt Sienna, Yellow, Country Blue, Flesh

INSTRUCTIONS:
Sand frame lightly including edges. Wipe carefully with cloth to remove dust. Using soft cloth, apply stain to front of frame. Trace pattern.

PAINT:
Outer and inner edges of frame - True Blue.
Transfer pattern.
Rainbow - Crimson, Pumpkin and Yellow.
Lettering - Black.
Cloud - Arctic White, outline Black.
Sun - Yellow.
  Cheeks - Carnation Pink, add small Arctic White dot.
  Eyes, mouth - Black.
Tree - Forest Green with Bright Green swirls.
  Apples - Crimson with Yellow highlight.
  Trunk - Burnt Sienna, outline Black.
Grass - Bright Green with Forest Green tufts.
Flowers - Yellow, dot centers Carnation Pink.
Giraffe - Pumpkin.
  Patches - Rust.
  Outline - Black.
Elephant - Slate Gray.
  Feet, inside ear - Carnation Pink. Shade outer edge of ear Black.
  Tail, eye - Black.
  Outline - Black.
Sheep - Slate Gray with Arctic Ice swirls.
  Eyes, legs, nose - Black.
Lion - Rust.
  Cheeks - Shade Crimson with Arctic White dot.
  Mane - Yellow swirls.
  Eyes, nose, mouth - Black.
  Outline - Black.
Noah
  Coat - Crimson with Yellow stripes.
  Head - Flesh.
  Cheeks - Carnation Pink with Arctic White dots.
Beard - Slate Gray with Arctic White swirls.
Eyes - Black.
Hands - Flesh.
Boots - Black, highlight Arctic White.
Outline - Black.
Bird - Country Blue, highlight Arctic White. Outline Black.
Ark - Pumpkin.
  Roof - Crimson.
  Bottom - Rust.
  Details - Black.
Mini sign - Pumpkin with Black lettering.
Canvas paper - Country Blue.
  Clouds - Arctic White.
Small birds - Black.

FINISH:
Spray with sealer. Glue paper to center back of opening and ark to bottom edge of center opening. Glue toothpick to Noah's hand and mini sign to toothpick. Drill small holes in top corners of frame. Thread wire through holes for hanger curling ends to hold wire in place. Tie jute bow to wire on top left corner.

Noah was building an ark
In the middle of Genesis Park
When the rain came to stay
He floated away,
Looking for somewhere to park!

Julie '96

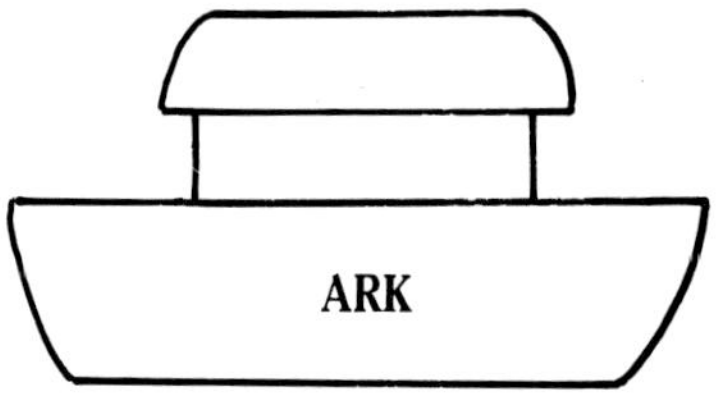

repared . . . it wasnt raining
when Noah built the ark

Garden Sampler

CENTER PHOTO

MATERIALS:

11" x 12½" Frame with a 3½" x 5" opening
3 mosquito birdhouses
Ribbon (Banner)
Medium primitive heart
Natural raffia
DecoArt Bleached Pine White Gel Stain
6" of 3/16" dowel
Ruler
24" of wire

ZIG WOODCRAFT MARKERS:

Big & Broad - Arctic White
Extra Fine - Black
Chisel Tip - Country Blue, Victorian Blue, Yellow, Rust, Crimson, Forest Green, Pumpkin, Carnation Pink, Violet

INSTRUCTIONS:

Sand frame if necessary, remove dust. Stain front of frame Bleached Pine White. Trace pattern.

PAINT:

Stripes - Using ruler and 2 to 3 coats, make Arctic White stripes the width of a Big & Broad Marker. Make Black stripes with Extra Fine Marker.
Transfer pattern.
Bird - Country Blue, shade Victorian Blue. Outline Black.
Sunflower - Yellow.
- Center - Rust, shade outside edge of center Rust.
- Cross hatch - Black, add Arctic White dots.
- Detail - stipple over shading lightly with Black. Outline Black.

Melon - Forest Green, Arctic White, Crimson.
- Seeds - Black.
- Lines between colors, outline - Black.

Carrots - Pumpkin, shade Rust. Highlight Yellow.
- Tops - Forest Green.

Gardening glove - Victorian Blue.
- Stripes - Country Blue.
- Heart - Crimson.

Sun - Yellow.
- Cheeks - Carnation Pink.
- Eyes, mouth - Black.
- Dashed line, outline - Black.

Pansy
- Outer petals - Violet.
- Inner petals - Arctic White.
- Outer edge - Country Blue.
- Center - shade Violet, dot Yellow.
- Outline - Black.

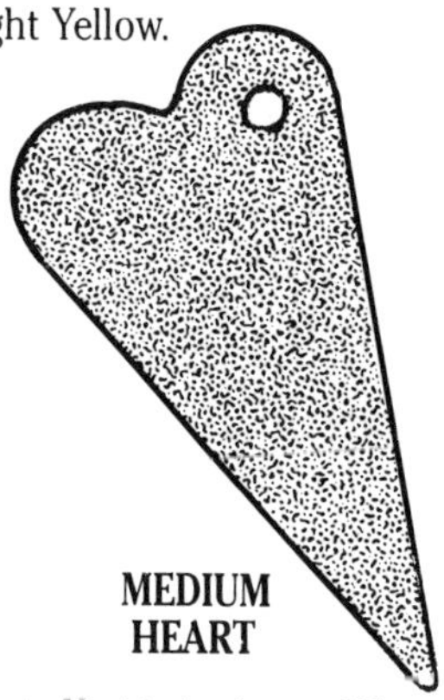

MEDIUM HEART

Watering can - Forest Green, shade Black. Highlight Arctic White.
Primitive heart - Crimson.
Ribbon - Forest Green, shade Black.
- Lettering - Arctic White.

Mosquito birdhouses - Crimson and Rust, Country Blue and Victorian Blue, Yellow and Forest Green. Add Arctic White dots.
Dowel - Forest Green.

FINISH:

Drill holes in bottom of mini birdhouses and 3 holes inside bottom edge of frame. Cut dowel into 1½", 2" and 2½" pieces, glue in mini birdhouses and holes in frame. Glue ribbon over top of center opening. Tie and glue a small raffia bow to each birdhouse. Drill a hole in top of primitive heart and top corners of frame. Wrap wire around ruler to shape center, thread ends through holes in top of frame from back to front and curl to secure. Spray with sealer. Tie raffia bow on top left corner. Attach primitive heart to end of wire.

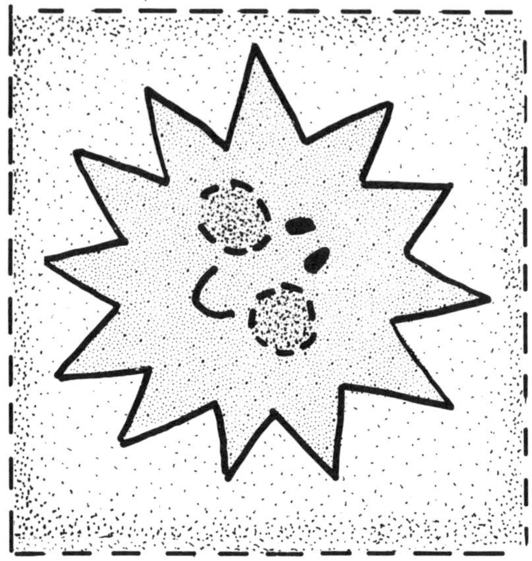

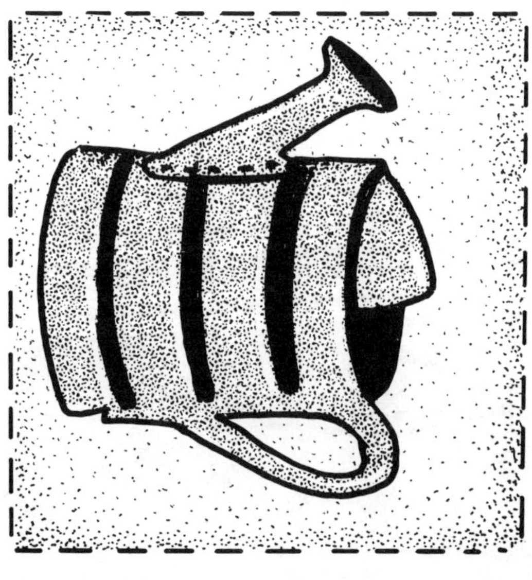

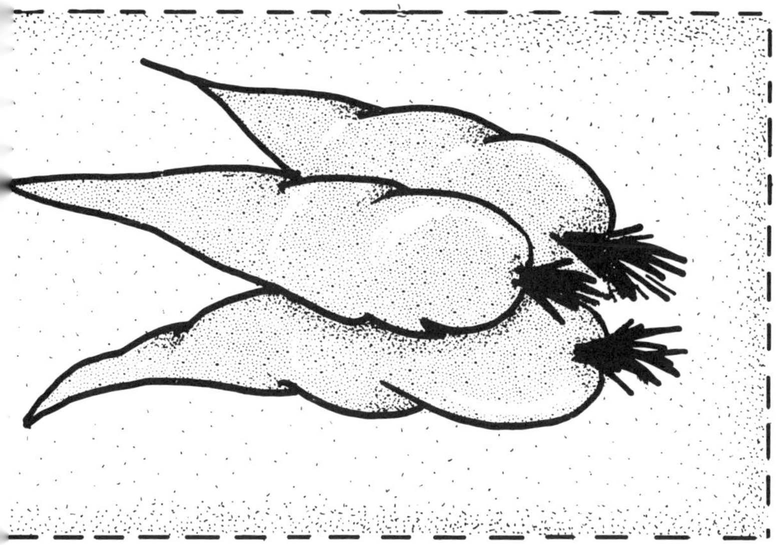

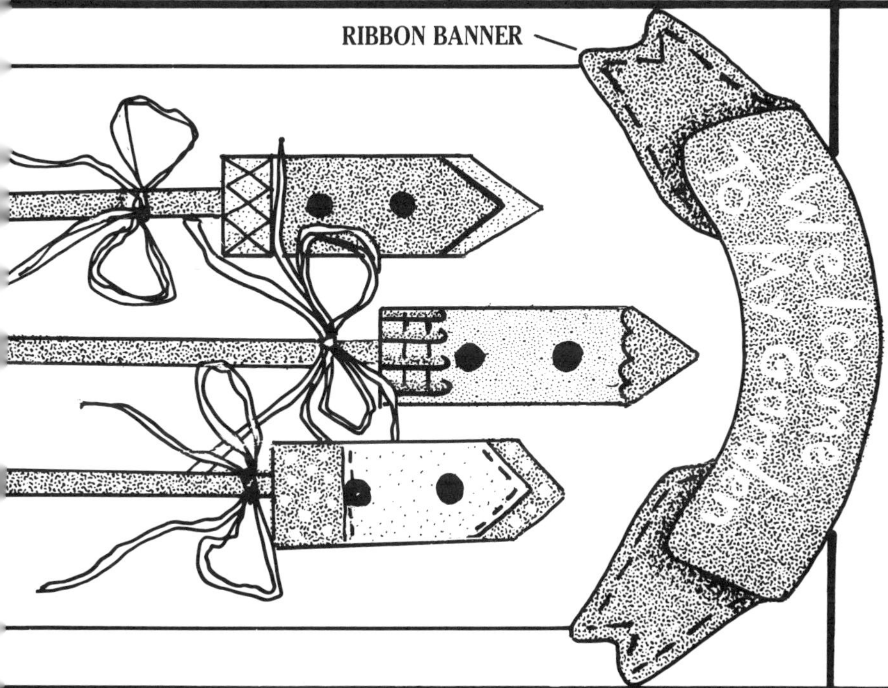
RIBBON BANNER
Welcome To My Garden

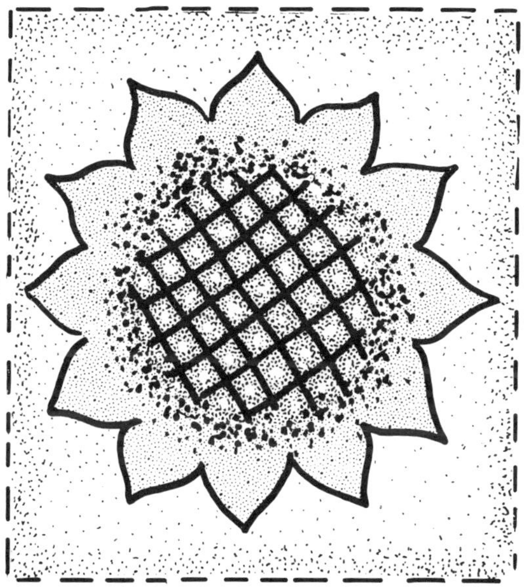

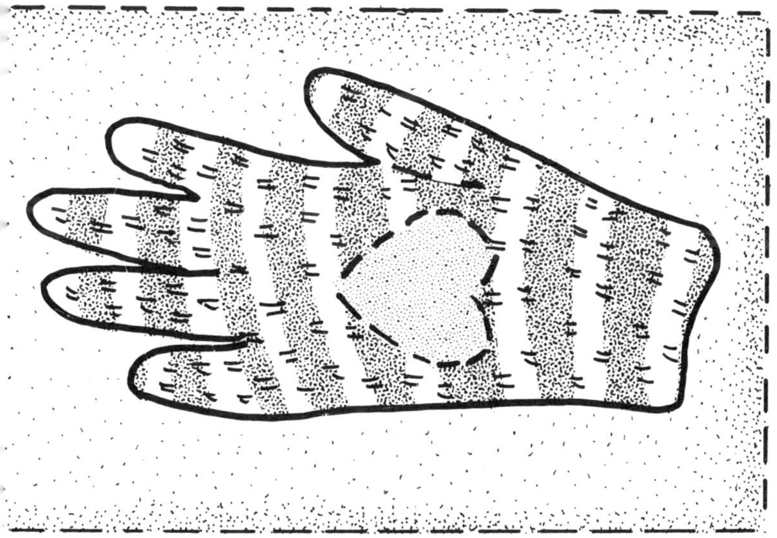

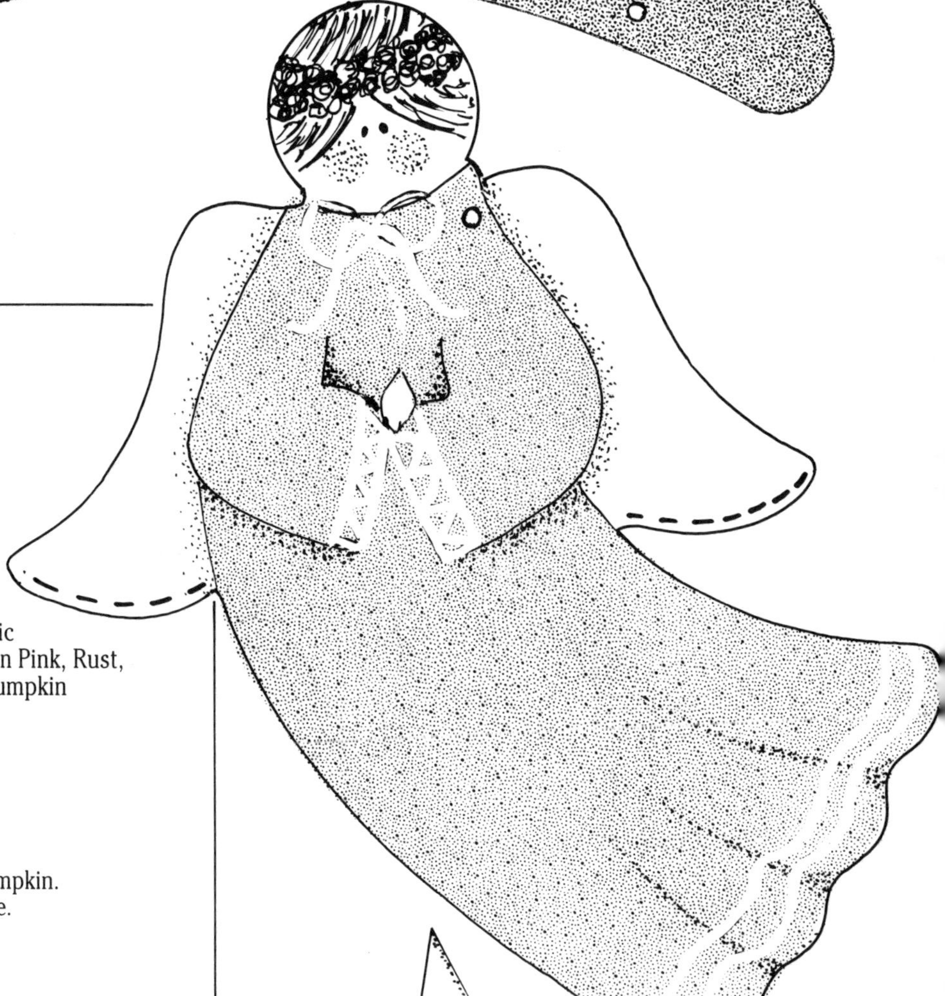

Starlight Angel

CENTER PHOTO

MATERIALS:
Wood 'n Wire banner
Flying angel ornament
Asymmetrical star ornament
3 small self adhesive stars
12" of Brass wire

ZIG WOODCRAFT MARKERS:
Big & Broad - True Blue
Extra Fine - Black, Arctic White, Gold Metallic
Chisel Tip - Peacock, Yellow, Flesh, Carnation Pink, Rust, Arctic White, Forest Green, Slate Gray, Pumpkin

INSTRUCTIONS:
Trace patterns.

PAINT:
Banner - True Blue.
Transfer patterns.
Small stars - Yellow.
Asymmetrical star - Yellow, shade edges Pumpkin.
- Cheeks - Carnation Pink, dot Arctic White.
- Eyes, mouth - Black.

Angel
- Head - Flesh.
- Cheeks - Carnation Pink, dot Arctic White.
- Eyes - dot Black.
- Hair - Yellow with Rust stripes.
- Garland - dot Forest Green, Carnation Pink, Arctic White and Yellow.
- Hands - Flesh.
- Dress - Peacock, shade True Blue.
- Wings - Arctic White, shade Slate Gray.
- Details on dress and wings, bow - Gold Metallic.

FINISH:
Cut wire in 4" and 8" pieces, curl around dowel. Attach long piece to angel and left side of banner. Attach short piece to asymmetric star and right side of banner. Glue star to angel. Spray with sealer.

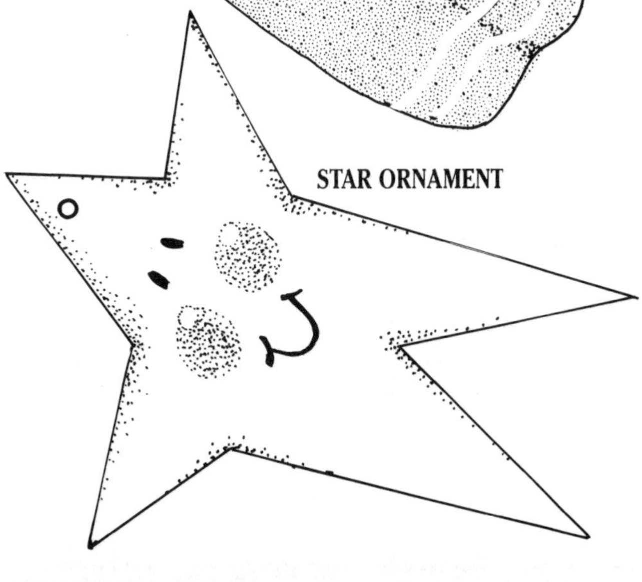

STAR ORNAMENT

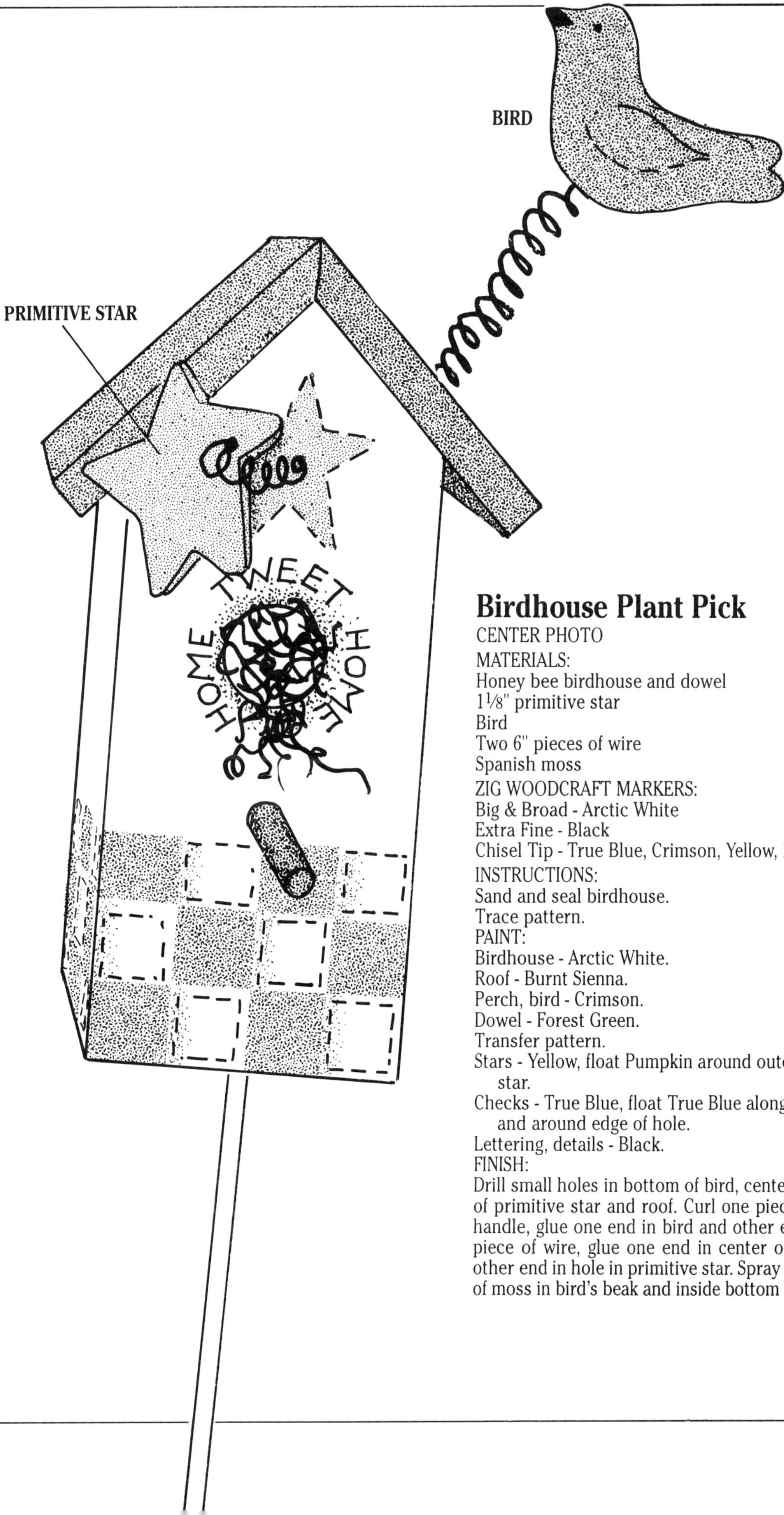

Birdhouse Plant Pick

CENTER PHOTO

MATERIALS:
Honey bee birdhouse and dowel
$1\frac{1}{8}$" primitive star
Bird
Two 6" pieces of wire
Spanish moss

ZIG WOODCRAFT MARKERS:
Big & Broad - Arctic White
Extra Fine - Black
Chisel Tip - True Blue, Crimson, Yellow, Pumpkin, Burnt Sienna.

INSTRUCTIONS:
Sand and seal birdhouse.
Trace pattern.

PAINT:
Birdhouse - Arctic White.
Roof - Burnt Sienna.
Perch, bird - Crimson.
Dowel - Forest Green.
Transfer pattern.
Stars - Yellow, float Pumpkin around outer edge of primitive star.
Checks - True Blue, float True Blue along one edge of checks and around edge of hole.
Lettering, details - Black.

FINISH:
Drill small holes in bottom of bird, center of star on house, edge of primitive star and roof. Curl one piece of wire around brush handle, glue one end in bird and other end in roof. Curl second piece of wire, glue one end in center of star on house. Secure other end in hole in primitive star. Spray with sealer. Glue strands of moss in bird's beak and inside bottom edge of hole.

Gardening Angel Plant Pick

CENTER PHOTO

WOOD PARTS:

Innkeeper Mini Sign
2 arms
Watering can
Mini primitive heart
Small apple (head)
Triangle body
$1\frac{1}{8}$" primitive star
1" heart (wings)

MATERIALS:

Spanish moss
Mini straw hat
Toothpick
12" of $\frac{3}{8}$" dowel

ZIG WOODCRAFT MARKERS:

Big Broad - Arctic White
Extra Fine - Black
Chisel Tip - Forest Green, Flesh, Crimson, Violet, Rust, Slate Gray, Yellow, Black

INSTRUCTIONS:

Trace patterns.

PAINT:

Sign - basecoat Arctic White, wash Rust. Border, dowel - Forest Green. Float Forest Green around border.
Transfer patterns.
Hearts - Crimson.
Primitive star - Yellow.
Stitch lines, lettering - Black.
Head, hands - Flesh.
Eyes, mouth - Black.
Sleeves, body - Crimson with Violet and Forest Green stripes.
Pinafore - Forest Green.
Watering can - Slate Gray, shade Black.
Wings - Arctic White, shade Rust.

FINISH:

Spray with sealer. Drill holes in bottom of star and sign and top of one hand. Assemble angel referring to photo, glue on sign. Glue dowel in bottom of sign.

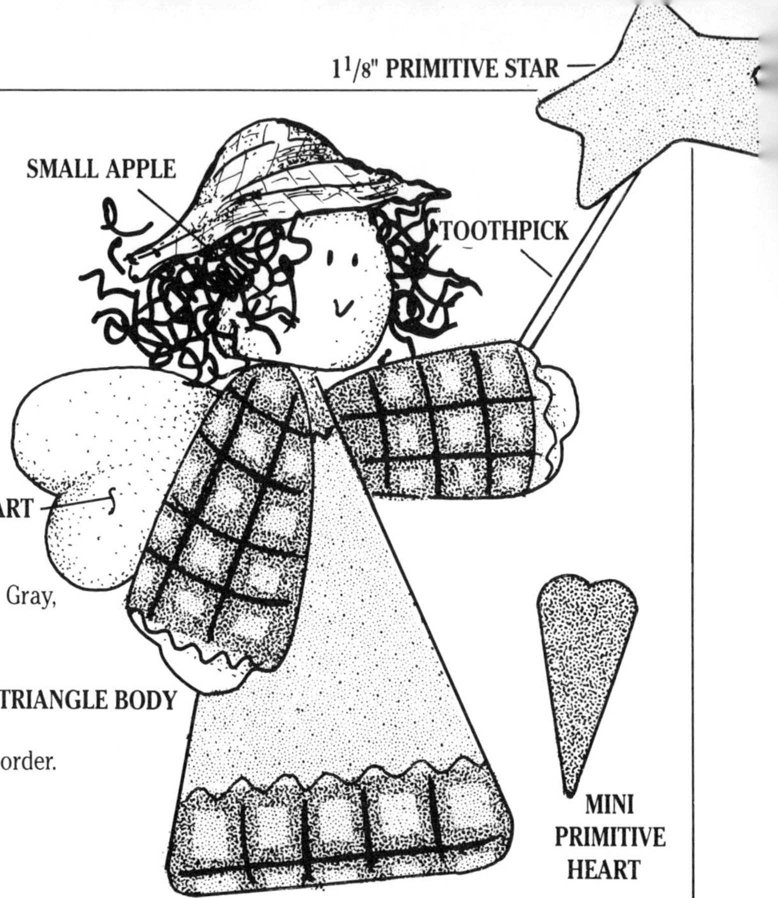

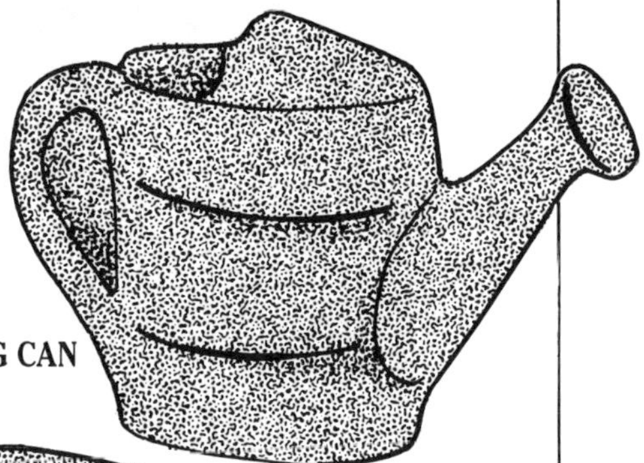

There is a little garden,
I tend with loving care
And if you ever look for me
You'll always find me there.
Planting seeds of happiness
Hoeing it with love
Watering it with Angel smiles
From the world above

Julie '96

Tomato Plaque

BACK COVER PHOTO

MATERIALS:
Rectangle mini sign
12" of wire
Raffia

ZIG WOODCRAFT MARKERS:
Big & Broad - Arctic White
Extra Fine - Black
Chisel Tip - Bright Green, Black, Crimson, Yellow, Forest Green, Rust, Pumpkin

INSTRUCTIONS:
Trace pattern.

PAINT:
Sign - basecoat edge Arctic White and center Bright Green.
Transfer pattern.
Checks - Black.
Corners - Crimson.
Tomatoes - Crimson, shade Rust. Highlight Yellow.
  Tops - Forest Green.
Banner - Yellow, shade underside Pumpkin.
  Lettering, outline - Black.

FINISH:
Drill holes in corners of sign, attach wire for hanger and curl ends to secure. Tie raffia bow on hanger.

Birds Drop Inn

BACK COVER PHOTO

MATERIALS:
Sunburst mini sign
Birdhouse
3/8" button
Small twig
Gray moss
9" of wire

ZIG WOODCRAFT MARKERS:
Extra Fine - Black, Gold Metallic
Chisel Tip - Country Blue, Arctic White, Forest Green, Rust, Crimson, True Blue

INSTRUCTIONS:
Trace pattern.

PAINT:
Sign - Country Blue, shade edge True Blue.
  Outline - Black dashes.
  Lettering - Black.
Transfer pattern.
Birdhouse - Arctic White.
  Roof - Forest Green, shade Rust.
  Stars - Gold Metallic, outline Black.
  Checks - Rust.
Button - Crimson.
  Center - Black.

FINISH:
Glue birdhouse to sign and button to center of birdhouse. Trim twig to appropriate size, glue to sign under birdhouse. Glue small ball of moss to twig. Spray with sealer. Attach wire to sign, curl ends to secure.

BIRDHOUSE

Santa Birdhouse Pick

CENTER PHOTO

MATERIALS:
Small Primitive Star
Mini Tall Triangle clock
9" of 3/8" dowel
Ribbon bow (mustache)
3/8" bead (bird)
Toothpick (beak)
Spanish moss
6" of wire

ZIG WOODCRAFT MARKERS:
Big & Broad - Crimson
Extra Fine - Black, Arctic White
Chisel Tip - Flesh, Arctic White, Black, Slate Gray, Yellow, Carnation Pink, Burnt Sienna

INSTRUCTIONS:
Trace and transfer pattern.

PAINT:
Hat, cape - Crimson, shade Black.
Boots - Black, highlight Arctic White.
Face - Flesh.
  Cheeks - Carnation Pink, dot Arctic White.
  Eyes - dot Black.
  Mouth - Burnt Sienna, outline Black.
Hole - Arctic White.
Fur - Arctic White, shade Slate Gray, detail Black.
Mustache - Arctic White, shade Slate Gray.
  Nose - Crimson.
Star - Yellow.
Dowel - Burnt Sienna.
Bird - Crimson.
  Eyes - dot Black.
  Beak - Black.

FINISH:
To make bird, glue end of toothpick in bead, cut to size. Drill small holes in top of clock and star. Drill hole in bottom of clock for dowel. Attach wire to star, curl and glue other end in hole at top of clock. Glue dowel in bottom of clock. Spray with sealer. Glue moss in hole and bird in moss.

Santa was feeling quite weird,
He cried, "It is just as I feared.
A sparrow, a wren,
A lark and a hen
Have just built a nest in my beard!"
Julie '96

3/8" BEAD

Here Birdie

BACK COVER PHOTO

MATERIALS:
Small arch garden sign
Bird
18" of Natural raffia
6" of wire

ZIG WOODCRAFT MARKERS:
Big & Broad - Arctic White
Extra Fine - Black
Chisel Tip - Rust, Carnation Pink, Peacock, Pumpkin, Yellow Forest Green, Crimson

INSTRUCTIONS:
Trace pattern.

PAINT:
Sign - basecoat Arctic White
  Edge, dowel - Forest Green. Float Yellow around edge then Rust. Transfer pattern.
Cat - Rust.
  Stripes, eyes, nose, mouth, whiskers - Black, shade Black.
Hearts - Crimson.
Flowers - Pumpkin, Carnation Pink and Peacock.
  Centers - Yellow, shade Rust.
Leaves, stems - Forest Green.
Flowers, leaves, hearts - outline Black.
Dashes, lettering - Black.
Bird - Crimson, float Black along wing and tail feathers.
  Beak - Yellow, outline Black.
  Eye - dot Black.

FINISH:
Spray with sealer. Drill small hole in bottom of bird and top of sign. Wrap wire around brush handle to curl. Glue one end in bottom of bird and other end in top of sign. Tie raffia bow around top of dowel, glue to secure.